Encounters

A journey into the heart of God

and His heart for you

by

Peter Waller

ENCOUNTERS

For our Treasures Ministry:

www.treasures.org.uk

treasures.org.uk@gmail.com

Ordering Information:

E-book and printed copies can be purchased through Amazon.

ISBN 9798653111228

Acknowledgments

For many years I have carried a dream and received many words about writing, but it was something I always put off. There was always a good reason to delay starting; I wasn't eloquent enough, wasn't time, lack of inspiration, not famous enough and so the list went on.

So thank you to Andy and Sharon Britton who created an environment in the church family that encouraged me to start walking a journey, to simply start writing and see where it might lead. So the dream that had been planted many years ago began to germinate.

Thank you to Lynn Strietzel who provided practical wisdom and guidance on the style of writing – so that this is not a book where you are being preached at! But rather a place of encounter.

Thank you to Karen, my precious and beautiful wife, who supported, loved, encouraged and helped me on this journey. You have modelled love so well and have helped me experience and understand it and so much more…

ENCOUNTERS

Endorsements

Wow! I felt like I just stepped out of the Bible. These stories are so "alive", I felt I was the main character in each story and the love Jesus had for each person who encountered Him is also the love He has for me.

First the Story then the questions then the blessings. No other book does this. This book is different. It has so much "life" in it you feel you are an actual person in each story. The Bible stories will come alive as you read. Peter has lived what he has written, one can tell because there is so much "life" flowing out of the way he tells the stories.

But these are not just stories, they are real encounters. Read for yourself and see. Read this book and you will enter into the heart of Jesus, the Father and the Holy Spirit.

Marla Baum, Leader of Bethel Church's
Apostolic Prophetic Intercessors, CA USA

Peter has written a remarkable little book. It is my unwavering experience that God speaks through scripture. Some of the nuances and understandings may have been lost through time and cultural changes and Peter has done a great job of bringing things back to life through his retelling of some of the familiar stories. He poses some challenging and deeply necessary questions. I was blessed in the retelling and so will you be.

Irvin Allen, Bethel Sozo Regional Facilitator UK

ENCOUNTERS

Peter is a man who has encountered and abides in the love of God. In the years that I have known him I have seen both Peter and his wife Karen demonstrate this love to those around them.

In this enjoyable and easy to read book Peter captures the readers imagination in a series of short stories based on ten ordinary people from the Gospels, who had life changing encounters with Jesus. Peter has creatively written their potential back stories and thought processes, thus highlighting their humanity. This wonderfully shows how everyday people, like ourselves, can have an encounter with Jesus, who loves us despite our human frailty.

Towards the end of each chapter Peter invites the reader to consider their own circumstances and encourages them to make space for their own encounter with the wonderful love of God.

Paula Jayne Bate, Paula Jayne Ministries UK

In "Encounters" Peter brilliantly transports the reader back to the raw real sights, sounds and smells of the character. We don't just imagine them, but we actually experience it with them! Then Peter brings the reader full circle as he masterfully draws the reader into an authentic adventure with the implication and application to the readers own personal life.

Lynn Strietzel, Author, Whispers of His Word

This is an excellent first book! It covers material covered by other writers before, but in a unique and refreshing way. Peter is very loyal to what is recorded in the Bible, but with creative imagination seeks to enter into the hearts of each individual who had a significant encounter with Jesus. The results are very moving and challenging. Peter writes in a very warm and expressive style, and encourages readers to expect similar life-changing encounters with the living Jesus today.

David Dominy, Retired Pastor, Stafford UK.

Peter has a wonderful ability to bring the Bible to life fostering fresh revelation of God's promises. Each account is paraphrased to help the reader comprehend the Biblical narrative from a new perspective.

Peter's notes encourage the reader to meditate on different aspects of God's character. He inspires us to respond to the Holy Spirit's bringing freedom and restoration.

David and Linda Perham, Stafford UK

ENCOUNTERS

Foreword

A few years ago Peter received a prophetic word from Isabel Allum, speaking of his character as being like that of Enoch, a man in the Bible who walked intimately and faithfully with God. (Genesis 5:24)

I truly feel privileged to write the foreword for Peter's first book, not simply because he is my husband, but because I know more than anyone who he truly is. I know his lifestyle of intimacy with God, his pure passion for God's Word and his love to teach others with a rare gift of emotive expression and authentic interpretation.

I believe an author's work flows from what they believe, but that their work carries the fragrance of who they truly are. Peter is a man who truly loves God and carries a rare fragrance of purity. The Bible says; "The pure in heart will see God," (Matthew 5:8 NIV) and he does.

Peter truly is a man who walks in a genuine humility each and every day in the seen and unseen of life. His love towards people is shown in his servant heart, his gentle and compassionate nature and his tender insight into the vulnerabilities of the human heart... all enfolded in such deep, rich wisdom and truth. This is the fragrance of Peter and it is the fragrance of 'Encounters'.

It will teach you, yes, but so much more... it will inspire you to enjoy and explore scripture in a new and real way, it will disarm you emotionally with its humility and kindness, unravelling those hidden emotions and painful places deep within. Yet, don't discard the gentleness for weakness, for Peter carries you safely and strongly as he invites you into the pure presence of a good and loving Father... A place where you can truly be known and loved, and begin to hear the healing words for your own story and experience your own breakthroughs too.

'Encounters' truly is that, a series of interpreted Biblical encounters that lead you into your own encounters with Love Himself, with Peter as the skilled guide taking you through each step.

So step aside a while, embrace a fresh humility to hear from God, open your heart and expect to be deeply changed... you will be.

Karen Waller

Table of Contents

ENCOUNTERS

Introduction

Just one moment, just one short encounter with Jesus was all it took for people to step into freedom, wholeness and life. That was all it took for them to get a break through, even after years of suffering with complex issues. Just one single moment with Jesus!

These ten stories are all based on the accounts found in the gospels but they are not meant to be read as scripture. However, they are written to be consistent with both God's and man's nature. By dramatizing the accounts, my hope is that they would help you experience just one possibility of what it might have been like for each person. A glimpse into the unique journey of their hearts and minds, of their hopes and fears, leading up to the moment of their encounter with Jesus and subsequent breakthrough.

Every story, every breakthrough, has been recorded in scripture to encourage us. For what God has done for one, is available for all... for you!

My prayer for you is that you too will have such a moment. When you put this book down and the words fade away, and you too personally encounter Jesus and be forever changed by His love. For His greatest desire is that you know in every fibre of your being, His love for you. And to enjoy Him for all eternity.

ENCOUNTERS

After each short story I have added a few thoughts and questions to help you ponder, explore and go on your own journey of encounters with Jesus.

Journey to the Well

The valley was dry and barren with just a few bits of scrub clinging to the rocky soil, hinting that there might still be some water flowing underground beneath the old river bed. The only movement was the shimmering of light caused by the heat of the mid-day sun. Nothing had moved for the last hour since a group of men had passed through, leaving one of their party lying in the shade under the old olive tree by the well.

It was the sound of a dislodged stone rolling down the hill that gave the first indication that someone was approaching. The traveller lying under the tree stirred, sat up and smiled. He looked tired but expectant.

In the town above the valley, all was quiet as everyone was resting in the shade from the hot mid-day sun. There was one exception though. On her own and carrying a water jar, Abigail headed down the long path to the well at the bottom of the hill. It was a painful journey for her, partly because of the oppressive heat, but more so because of the memories.

Passing by the cave where as a young woman she had gone with James. How he had whispered so seductively to her that he would love her forever, making so many promises of what their life would be like. Ha! It wasn't even a year before he told her to leave because he'd found someone else.

ENCOUNTERS

Continuing to wind her way down the path she paused, resting her hand on the olive tree where Matthew had proposed to her. Outrageous, impetuous Matthew. The only man she had ever known truly loved her and whom she truly loved. So often reckless but how he had loved life and helped her to believe for more.

They had barely had two short happy years before that fateful day, when mending the roof, he fell off and broke his neck. The searing pain pierced her once again. The tears had long since dried up but the ache in her heart, though dulled at times, had never gone away. Would it ever be possible to be freed from the pain and loss she wondered? To be able to truly feel loved again.

There had been other men with their sweet words and a promise of a future together. Only to be followed by yet more pain, either from death or betrayal. Not that she was always the innocent one she mused. The thorn bush had long since recovered from when Joanna and her had tumbled into it. That was when Joanna had confronted and attacked her after discovering she was the reason Simon was leaving.

Strange how the cuts and bruises on the outside could heal so quickly, but those wounds on the inside never seemed to heal. Since that day she had been an outcast and not welcomed with the other women of the village when they went to get water in the cool of the day. So now in the heat, all alone, she trudged down the path to the well.

Preoccupied with her own thoughts, it was only when she turned the last corner in the path and looked up that she saw the traveller sitting in the shade under the old olive tree, looking at her. She paused and for a moment there was an irrational urge to run away. She was alone out here with no-one to protect her. What if something happened? But she needed the water.

Looking again there was something about the relaxed way the stranger was resting that was unthreatening. Even so, best to keep the well between them. Avoiding eye contact, Abigail slowly approached the well and reached down to move the roughhewn stone that covered the well. The base of the stone had become smooth over the centuries and slid easily enough to the side, releasing the smell of cool refreshing damp air. As she started to lower her water jar to draw water the traveller spoke.

"Woman, please may I have a drink of water?"

For a moment she froze. The man was a Jew! To drink, he would have to use her bucket. No self-righteous Jew would ever do that! What was he after? Yet there was no animosity or arrogance in his voice, just a simple request. Who was this weird and bizarre Jewish man?

"You are a Jew and I am a Samaritan woman. How can you ask me for a drink?" She challenged.

"If you knew who I am, and the gift God has for you, you would be asking me to give you living water" He confidently said.

Living water? she wondered looking around. The only fresh water within miles of here was at the bottom of this well and clearly the stranger had no bucket of his own. Who was this man with his strange claim but gentle voice?

"Sir, the freshwater is deep down and you don't have a bucket. Where are you going to get this living water from? It was our father

Jacob who dug this well. Drinking its water gave him life and life to all his family and livestock. Are you claiming to be greater than Jacob?"

The stranger smiled. It seemed such a natural open smile Abigail thought, as an ache stirred within her heart, he must smile a lot. Pointing to the well the man said. "Everyone who drinks from this well gets thirsty again". Then turning and looking her in the eyes he continued, "Those who drink from the water I give will never be thirsty again. Indeed, the water I give will become a spring of water that wells up inside of them giving them eternal life".

What? Never be thirsty again? That's impossible! His words didn't make any sense. He was probably mad or suffering from heat stroke, best ignore him and turn away. Yet when she looked again into his eyes she shivered, these were not the eyes of a madman. They were too 'clear', too 'open', too... seeing! His voice was gentle but he spoke with such confidence and authority, somehow she sensed there was truth in what he said. To cover her confusion, she focused on pulling up the filled water jar.

She had challenged him, but now his words were challenging her. Could it really be possible that there was water you could drink and then never be thirsty again? If so she would never have to face this journey to the well again. Who was this man with such an incredible claim? There was a risk she would look a fool but she was long past caring what others thought. The possibility of never being thirsty again was too valuable to ignore in this God-forsaken, dry and parched land.

"Sir, please give me some of this water, then I will never be thirsty or have to come down here for water again".

For a moment he looked at her, as if to weigh the strength of her desire. "Go and get your husband, then come back".

She looked down as she felt his words pierce to the very core of her heart. Get her husband? if only she could have! To receive and share such a gift of life together as one! It was all she had ever wanted, to have a husband and family, to belong. But Reuben was out of town, yet again, and it could be days before he came back...

"I have no husband" she said, as pain from the past stirred afresh in her heart.

"Very true, you do indeed have no husband" the man said gently. "In fact, you've had five husbands and the man you now have is not your own husband".

He knew her past! Her mind raced as events and choices she had made flashed before her, pain and shame rose up within. She could feel her face beginning to burn. He knew all about her. He must have known it all along. He's a prophet!

She felt exposed, vulnerable, and yet amidst the swirling of emotions and thoughts, his eyes held her like an anchor. There was no condemnation, nor judgement here, but rather love and acceptance. Now it was her heart that burned within her as the revelation hit her. She was both known and accepted. Was it possible to be fully known and yet also fully loved and fully accepted by God too? Besides who was this Prophet that showed such love?

As his words washed through her a longing grew deep within, oh to be able to know such a God! Even as hope was being birthed, the past would not be so easily brushed aside. Like a spectre it rose up before her, painfully mocking her, spitefully accusing her.

"Where could a woman like you ever go to meet with God? You're rejected by the Jews for being a Samaritan, and rejected by your own people because of the woman you are!"

But despite this, hope had been born and it would not be denied.

"Sir, I can see you are a prophet. Our ancestors worshipped on this mountain, but you Jews claim that the place we must go to in order to worship God is in Jerusalem."

"Believe me precious woman, a time is coming when you will worship the Father neither on this mountain nor in Jerusalem".

You will worship... You will worship... The words resounded within her. This was a promise and she drank it in. She could, indeed she would worship! To be able to worship anywhere, not having to go to a special place. But to worship God as Father? What did that mean?

"You Samaritans worship what you do not know, for salvation is from the Jews. But the time is coming, indeed it is now here, when the true worshippers will worship the Father in spirit and truth. For these are the people the Father seeks as his worshippers. For God is spirit and the people who worship him must do so in spirit and truth."

She felt her mind being stretched and pulled as she strained to understand the truth she knew was there but still not quite able to grasp it. Yet his words were also speaking to something deeper within, at the very core of her identity, something was being awakened.

Her mind flashed back to a moment, decades ago when she was a little girl sitting with her grandmother one evening watching the sun set. "Grandma, have you ever seen God?" She'd asked. Grandma had always talked about God like he was really there.

"No Abigail I haven't. Though I do see something of what he is like when I look around me, like in this beautiful sunset, or in a kind deed. But one day a special prophet, the Messiah, will come from God who will show us who God really is. I doubt that I will be alive when he comes now sweetheart, but I'm praying that one day you will get to meet him". "I would really like that," Abigail said as she snuggled in closer into her grandmother's arms.

Tears that had long since dried up began to well up and flow again. If only the Messiah was here she thought, he would be able to explain everything to her.

"I know that one day the Messiah is coming and he will explain everything to us".

In a voice that was both tender and yet triumphant, the man said, "I am he".

I am he...?

I AM!

YAHWEH!

YAHWEH, her heart sang...

YAHWEH, her spirit soared...

YAHWEH, her mind cried out...

YAHWEH, the Messiah!

Every fibre of her being vibrated with this revelation of Truth. Truth so real that the world around seemed but like a dream. For a moment as she looked into his eyes time and eternity joined as the Truth sank deep into her. The knowledge of the reality that the infinite God, who was all powerful, all present, all knowing, was also all loving and accepted and cared about her, just as she was!

How long she stood there she did not know. Gradually she became aware that a group of Jewish men had arrived and were standing to the side. Absently she noticed their looks of disapproval. She laughed! It didn't matter, it didn't matter anymore... not like before when her heart was hard and bitter. The knowledge that she was fully known, accepted and loved by God made it totally irrelevant what others thought.

This was good! This was indeed good news! As she thought of her own people, the compassion she had seen in his eyes welled up within her like a fountain. This was too good to keep to herself, she needed to share it. Leaving the water jar lying forgotten at her feet, she turned and ran up the path, laughing freely and filled with joy.

Based on John 4

Jesus reveals so well our Father God's heart of Love. His priority is always to make connection and relationship, but Love never forces itself, rather it invites. When we choose to respond to Love's invitation with an open heart, then Love reaches into us and draws us closer into deeper intimacy with himself. It is from this safe place of intimacy that we can receive the Truth about God and ourselves, and so step into the freedom and breakthrough that Truth brings.

Conversely if we reject Love's invitation, we end up moving away from Love into fear and ultimately hardening our hearts not only to Love's revelation but also to those who have chosen to embrace His invitation.

Love invites a response...

By asking the Samaritan woman for something that was well within her ability to do, He provided her with an opportunity to respond to Him, and so to open up and receive Love. Yes, there was a social taboo to step over, but nevertheless it was a simple enough request. I believe she responded because, despite everything, her heart was wanting and open to Love.

Take a moment to listen with new ears to the whispers of love that Father is speaking.

What is the invitation He is giving you, and what is your response?

Freedom through intimacy not understanding...

The Samaritan woman did not understand what Jesus meant by living water. So later in the conversation when she does ask Him for this living water she is expecting to receive physical water that will continually quench her physical thirst. But because her heart was open to Him and to what she thought He meant she actually received what He did mean. It's not about gaining greater understanding, but rather through greater intimacy that we step into freedom.

Is there something that you are struggling to understand but sense God is speaking to you about?

ENCOUNTERS

What can your heart say yes to?

Power of Truth when spoken in Love...

We are created in the image of God, who is the Truth, to have truth in the centre of our being. That truth will then be lived out and so shape our lives. Love does confront to expose the lies and reveal truth, but it does so within the context of a safe connection and relationship.

> *What truth is Father revealing to you that's exposing lies you've been believing about Him, about yourself or about others?*

> *Three simple steps in response;*
> *I repent for agreeing with the lie that ...*
> *I break agreement with the lie that ...*
> *I choose to believe the truth that ...*

> *What are the words/pictures of life He is giving that you can embrace and meditate on?*

The question that God IS answering...

I'm sure you've noticed that God doesn't always give us the answers to every question we ask Him. However, quite often it is the question behind the questions He answers. So for example, the question as to where you should go to worship God was probably one of the areas of greatest contention between the Jews and the Samaritans. Yet for both groups the focus was on a limited, finite, geographical location. A specific place where one had to first go to, before one could meet with God.

Jesus never answers her question as to "where" to worship. Instead He gives her a promise that she "will" worship. Which is why I think the real desire of her heart was actually to meet with God. But she believed, like so many others, that this could only take place in the right place. It's also interesting that when Jesus said "you will worship", he used the plural you rather than a singular you. He was also promising her that she would also be worshiping with others, would be part of a worshiping community, a place of belonging where she would no longer be excluded.

Does it feel like God is silent?

Spend some time quietly listening to God and let Him show you the question He IS answering.

Let this become the basis of moving forward.

A Prayer of Blessing…

In Jesus name I bless you to know that you are loved: That Almighty God, who is all knowing, all powerful and all present, is also all loving and completely accepts and embraces you as you are. With a never ending, always and forever love.

I bless you to know that you are fully known, fully loved and fully accepted by Him. That you are valued and treasured. That you are the apple of His eye, His delight and joy. You are the pearl of great price that He gave up everything for.

ENCOUNTERS

I bless you to hear His voice, to catch His heartbeat. To be confident in what you hear and to receive His love. I give you permission to not always have to understand but to trust in His goodness.

I bless you to be able to recognise, embrace and accept truth when you hear it. To know through encounter and experience the Love that surpasses knowledge. I declare that Truth Himself will work in you and bring you into freedom and an ever increasing greater revelation of Jesus, and who He created you to be.

Forgiven

For the umpteenth time Barak sighed as he lay there, all alone in the room, listening to the sounds drifting in from outside. He could hear the laughter of some children playing on the road. There was the chip, chip, chip as old Timaeus was chiselling away on some bit of wood. Then further away in the distance the scraping of a boat being pulled up onto the gravel stones by the shore as some fisherman worked on it. But his world had been reduced to this darkened room. Gone forever was the freedom to walk or run, to work and earn his own way.

Since the accident, his lot in life was reduced to relying on others and being a burden. He could not even go out and beg without someone carrying him. Of course he was grateful for his family and friends, they really were very good to him, but deep inside his heart ached with weariness. What was the point of living anymore?

Hearing excited voices, he turned his head as the door burst open and in rushed David. "Barak, Barak, Jesus of Nazareth has come back home again!" he exclaimed. "Now's our chance, Dan's gone to get Eli and we're going to carry you over to Jesus's house. You are going to be healed!"

Their words were like needles piercing the cloud of hopelessness he felt. "Are you sure, David? I don't want to be a bother. It's quite a way to carry me and Jesus will probably be coming down this way later."

"Barak, you're not a bother, you're a brother!" said Eli bursting with excitement as he came in with Dan. "I don't know why you're so reluctant. Jesus has healed plenty of people, even those who were born blind and deaf! So he can easily fix that back and those legs of yours again. So let's all get going!"

Swaying in the blanket hung between the two poles, all Barak could see was the clear blue sky over head and hear the excited chatter of his friends while they carried him along the road. But gradually their excitement grated his nerves. He'd heard all the stories about Jesus of Nazareth and knew it was possible that he could be healed, and indeed he did want to be healed, but they didn't know the truth about the cause of the accident.

Indeed, no one knew the real reason about why he had been there when the accident happened. What it was he had really been intending to do. It was all his own stupid fault. Why should he be healed when there were so many others far more deserving than himself? After all, the Pharisees were always telling them that if you disobeyed the law then you'd be judged by God. So now here he was paying the price for all his sins. His heart once again fell back into hopelessness and shame as he swung back and forth in his cocoon.

"Wow, look at that crowd outside the house. It will take some pushing and shoving to get through that lot!"

"Let's try round the back first."

"No it's just as bad here."

"Thanks for trying guys, why don't you just put me down somewhere out the front. I can always wait for Jesus to come out."

"Nonsense Barak, we've not carried you all this way just to leave you outside. There has to be a way in!"

"If ya can't go through, and ya can't go round, then ya have to go over I say!"

"What about those stairs to the roof? Have a quick look up there Dan and see if you can at least see whereabouts Jesus is sitting."

"There may even be some stairs going down inside that will at least get us into the courtyard. If I have to, I'd walk on top of every one of those people to get you to Jesus!"

"No, there's no stairs going down, but I can see through some lattice work where Jesus is. Bring him up and we will make a hole through the roof there and lower him down."

It was unnerving being lowered through the hole into the darkness below. Barak felt like he was sinking into a deep dark well, not knowing what awaited him. Once lying on the floor, all he could see was the small patch of bright blue sky above, it seemed so far away. He could feel his heart pounding in his chest and felt so small, helpless and vulnerable just lying there. In the darkness around he could sense the crowds of people but could not yet make out any details.

Gradually his eyes grew accustom to the dim light as out of the gloom a man approached and looked up at his four grinning friends. Then looking down at him, the man smiled. He had the clearest eyes Barak had ever seen. He quickly looked away feeling uncomfortable this must be Jesus of Nazareth. He really did want to be healed but the guilt weighed heavy in his heart. It was simply that he knew he just didn't deserve to be healed.

"Son, your sins are forgiven."

What? Forgiven! For a moment Barak was stunned.

He had been expecting Jesus to have waved his hand over him or say some special prayer, or to loudly expose his mistakes, challenge his hopelessness or confront his guilt and shame. But to simply say… forgiven?

The pain in his heart welled up. Actually the more he thought about it, he realised that forgiveness was what he truly wanted the most of all! Nobody had understood that his greatest pain was the guilt he felt in his heart, that it wasn't just his body that had been crippled…

He'd kept that secret hidden so well. Yet even though this man had seen it straight away he met his guilt and shame with grace and mercy. Hot tears flowed down his face. If only it was true that he could really be forgiven. But only God can do that and he'd already offered many sacrifices after the accident, hoping to be forgiven and get better - all to no avail, for the guilt and shame had still remained. If God had wanted to heal him then he would have already done it. Yet how his heart ached, still yearning for release, to be truly forgiven and be free. If only…

"… but I want you to know that the Son of Man has authority on earth to forgive sins." Jesus was saying to someone. Then turning back to Barak, he said "I tell you, get up, take your mat and go home."

Barak felt like fire exploded from within his heart, and the fear, guilt and shame were consumed in its raging blaze. He felt lifted up as the weight of it all was burnt away, he felt so light. Then as the fire shot down his legs and feeling returned, he felt like he was actually floating. In fact, the ceiling was coming nearer!

What? He was standing?!

Looking down at his legs, that moments ago had been wasted away, now they were strong and straight. He wobbled, leaning forward and took a step, his legs worked! Wow! Step by step, each one was a delicious experience of freedom and joy, to be savoured and cherished. God had healed him! Oh how precious, how glorious it was to walk again. Now tears of joy were streaming down his face. Laughing, he bent down and picked up his mat. Then stood up. Never before had he felt such joy in that simple act. He felt that he might burst!

The crowd parted before him as he walked out into the bright sun light.

Freed! Able to breathe again! To live again! To hope again!

Everyone was pointing at his legs and praising God. His friends had come down off the roof and were going wild, dancing, hugging everyone and praising God too. But Barak knew by far the greatest miracle had been the healing of his crippled heart. To finally be free from all that guilt, shame and condemnation. It was beyond words. To know that he had truly been forgiven, that was the greatest gift of all.

How on earth was it possible that God had given a man such authority to forgive sins, when all the sacrifices of animals prescribed in the Law of Moses had not been able to achieve it. What possible sacrifice could ever have been great enough to allow this, and who on earth could have possibly paid it?

Based on Mt 9, Mk 2 and Lk 5

Having studied with a number of different inner healing ministries over the years, there are two foundational important truths that they are all based on: Firstly, to minister in love so that people encounter love and leave loved. Secondly, helping them to come to a place of knowing they are forgiven, and releasing forgiveness to those who have hurt them.

Love without measure...

Think on this a moment: What could possibly be of value to God, when He can do anything and create anything simply with a word? What is it that could actually be a cost to God?

He gave Himself, this is the value He places on you! Your worth and identity are not defined by your actions, be they either good works or any failures or sin. Your value is measured by the sacrifice that God paid for you and the relationship with Himself that He has consequently brought you into.

If that makes you feel uncomfortable, please don't rush on. Take a moment to acknowledge the discomfort before Him, but also face and receive the incredible truth of how deeply to which He values you! In it you will find healing, freedom and life.

The cross showed the full extent of our Father's love for us. Though our sin is finite, Father God paid without measure, because His love is without measure.

Spend some time meditating on this, for there is courage and strength in this for the journey into wholeness.

Receiving the gift of forgiveness...

Whether it was because the paralytic man believed that God hadn't forgiven him, or that he hadn't forgiven himself, we don't know. However, the fact that Jesus's initial response to the man was to declare "your sins are forgiven", implies to me that this must have been what the man needed to hear the most. This was the key for him. Embracing this truth meant he would be able to come into freedom within his heart, which then became manifest in the healing of his body.

Sometimes it's only after we are able to step into the place of knowing that we have truly been forgiven, or choosing to forgive others or even ourselves, that we become positioned to receive and walk in the full healing or breakthrough that we are seeking.

Is there an area of your life where you still "feel guilt or shame"? Or where you need to hear Father's assurance that you are fully forgiven, accepted and embraced? Meditate on these scriptures...

***Jeremiah 31:3 NIV** The LORD appeared to us in the past, saying: "I have loved you with an everlasting love; I have drawn you with unfailing kindness. "*

***Isaiah 43:25 NET** "I, I am the one who blots out your rebellious deeds for my sake; your sins I do not remember."*

John 3:16 NET For this is the way God loved the world: He gave his one and only Son, so that everyone who believes in him will not perish but have eternal life.

Romans 3:23-24 NIV for all have sinned and fall short of the glory of God, and all are justified freely by his grace through the redemption that came by Christ Jesus.

Giving the gift of forgiveness ...

When feeling the pain of an injustice we can be tempted to believe that it's not until we see justice satisfied, by judgement being declared and carried out on the one who hurt us, that we will we be able to move on and find peace. Another belief is that forgiveness implies it didn't matter, but these are not the case.

When we choose not to forgive, we are holding someone accountable to us and judging them. However, the law we are using to condemn others, will ultimately end up condemning us. In judging we also remain bound to the pain that was experienced. We become bound by those bitter root judgements.

In choosing to release forgiveness, however, we hand over the role of judge to Father God, who is good and knows all and sees all. We then become free and positioned to encounter His love and peace in the place of our hurt and pain. The wounds, no matter how deep or old, can then be healed by His love.

One aspect of forgiveness involves letting go. Is there something that Jesus is inviting you to let go of?

ENCOUNTERS

I invite you to visualise Him standing in front of you right now, with open arms, and release this to Him.

Forgiveness also involves receiving too. Ask Jesus to show you what He is giving you in return.

Forgiving ourselves...

We are all aware of the need to forgive others, but equally we need at times to forgive ourselves. When we make decisions that hurt or harm us, it is as much a violation as if it was someone else doing it to us.

If you carry anger, hurt, resentment or frustration towards yourself, I invite you to speak forgiveness aloud over yourself.

Staying in Hope, resisting hopelessness...

When we believe that there is going to be a breakthrough our hope can be strong, for we see it can happen. But if time passes and the "facts" remain unchanged, it's harder to believe that there will be a change and hopelessness can start to grow. When logic, reason and our emotions are presenting undeniable "facts", then is the time to go back to the "truth", what God has said. This is the truth to embrace and declare for this truth will set us free.

A Prayer of Blessing...

In Jesus name I bless you to know that you have been fully and completely forgiven by God. That before Jesus created you, He foresaw your whole life and knew every decision and choice you would ever make. Knowing all this He loved you and chose to forgive you, to die for you and to create you.

I bless you to know the joy that Jesus had as He endured the pain of the cross, the joy of becoming one with you! Just as He was one with the Father. I bless you with the joy of intimacy with God, of knowing you are fully embraced and accepted.

I bless you with the joy of forgiving others, to release them to Daddy God so that you can walk free. To live free from the bondages of un-forgiveness and be empowered to become all He created you to be. I bless you to be able to know, and to live, Love.

I bless you to experience and know shalom, the peace and wholeness that comes from being one with God. Of being totally embraced, accepted and loved by Him. I bless you to rest in His faithfulness towards you.

I bless you with outrageous hope! That joyful expectation in the goodness of God. I bless you with a hope that is rooted in the truth that Papa God is speaking over you. That His words become so real inside of you they burst forth bringing about the breakthrough.

Made Whole

The woman stood alone. Half hidden amongst the rocks and scrub by the side of the cliff, she was panting and out of breath.

Looking down to the lake shore she groaned seeing the crowds congregating below.

Earlier, when the runner had come through Capernaum, she was fortunate to have been in the right place to overhear the news that the Rabbi was coming back home. Now was her chance! Heading off straight away she had hoped to be the first to meet him. But it had proved to be a vain hope, for she'd had to come the back way and down by the shore the crowds were already gathering as the boats approached.

There would be many there who would recognise her on sight. How on earth was she going to get to meet Jesus of Nazareth with so many people around? There was no way she could risk being seen by going down there! So she waited, hoping and praying that an opportunity would arise. Yet all the time knowing in her heart that the crowds would never leave him alone.

Hearing a commotion from behind, she turned quickly and saw Jairus, the synagogue leader coming down the path. Fear gripped her. If he saw her out here in public he would denounce her, then the crowd might turn on her and stone her. Quickly she ducked down behind a bush and waited, watching as Jairus, without any hesitation, went and pushed his way straight through the gathering crowds to speak to Jesus.

She strained to listen but couldn't hear what they were saying above the murmur of voices. After a moment, Jesus turned aside and headed back up the path with Jairus, followed by the ever growing crowd.

Her heart sank like a stone, for now any possibility of her being able to get alone with Jesus was totally lost. The crowd was starting to head her way and she would have to get out of there quickly. The pain of yet another disappointment cut deep.

For twelve horrible long years she had suffered. No one had been able to help her. Neither doctors, nor priests. No matter what she tried, it just kept getting worse. Now her one last hope, the miracle-working Rabbi, Jesus, was also out of reach. Hopelessness descended over her like a smothering blanket, disgusting her and yet feeling so familiar.

It had not always been like this. Once she had been well-known, a woman of beauty and significance. One to be admired. But now she was simply known as "that unclean woman!" or just "Ugh, its unclean!". Broken and destitute, her body racked in pain, she felt dirty, smelly, ugly. If only she could have been touched by Jesus, she knew she would have been healed. That's how Elizabeth and Salome were healed; they reached out their hands and he touched them as he walked past. Why was life so hard for her?

Touched? Touch! The thought suddenly exploded within her. What if she just touched him? After all a touch was a touch regardless who started it. Could she risk it? Perhaps with the shawl over her head no-one would notice her in the crowds. After all they would be totally focused on Jesus. Maybe she could slip in and out without anyone knowing, it might work!

Torn between fear and hope she stood there, rooted to the spot in indecision as the crowds started to pass by. Now Jesus was opposite her and she had to quickly make a choice. Everything felt twisted inside of her, why was it all so hard? In a moment he would pass by and be gone forever. It was either now or never!

Arghhh... Yes!!!!

Lifting the shawl up over her head, and with her heart pounding within her chest, she stepped out and plunged into the crowd. Immediately she felt swallowed up, drowning in the heaving mass of people pressing around her on all sides. Never had she been touched like this. It made her skin crawl. The smell of sweaty bodies was disgusting, she wanted to gag, to get out and run as far away as possible, to hide. She could feel panic beginning to rise.

Yet there was also a place in her heart that had now become focused and calm. Deep down within, indecision had been replaced by a choice and an action, and with the action her hope was growing stronger. Just touch his cloak, that's all I need to do she thought. I will be healed. Just touch his cloak.

Pressing in she reached out her hand, only to have someone push it away as they moved in front of her. Again and again, jostling with the flow of the crowds around him. It was like a dance, moving closer, then being pushed back. Like the rolling of the waves, back and forth, back and forth. But the steps didn't matter in this dance. Just the focus, to reach out and touch. To keep going!

Yes, another gap… and… touched!

Then she felt it, power surged up her arm and into her body! Like the gushing forth of a mighty fountain of water, going deep down inside and she knew instantly that she was healed. The flow of blood stopped.

Now to quickly slip out before she was discovered. She tried to turn, but the crowds that had reluctantly given way coming, now pressed back and blocked her.

"Who touched my clothes?"

She froze. That was the Rabbi Jesus, he knew he'd just been touched! Of course he would! He's a prophet! How stupid she had been to think she could get away with it! She pulled the shawl tighter over her head and ducked down even lower.

"Who touched me?"

The crowds moved uneasily around him but the press of those behind her now completely blocked her escape, they were an impenetrable wall, she was trapped! She couldn't see Jesus but for a moment she caught the look on Jairus's face through a gap in the crowd. Fear griped her for he would certainly denounce her!

"Who touched me?"

Feeling sick to the pit of her stomach, she knew that she was going to be exposed. Yes, she had been healed but at what cost? To have come into the crowd, an unclean woman! To have touched so many people, to even have touched and made the Rabbi Jesus unclean!

"Who touched me?"

"Master there's a crowd pressing around us? Why are you asking who touched you?"

"Who touched me?"

The unease in the crowd grew as those closest to him now tried to step back. There was no getting away, trembling with fear, she stepped forward and falling down at his feet, head bowed, she confessed all. The hurt and pain, the loss and the shame all rose up within her. She had been healed, but she had also broken the law. So now she waited for the condemnation and judgement that would swiftly follow.

There was silence. No one moved. Then she felt a hand gently touch the side of her face, Jesus's hand. Oh so gentle, that she yielded to his touch and looked up, and for the first time saw his eyes... his love for her...

"Daughter, your faith has healed you. Go in peace."

The words washed over her, through her, around her, in her. The great heavy load that had clung to her for so long was lifted off and she felt for the first time completely clean. Peace flooded every fibre of her being, going even deeper than where the healing power had flowed. She knew she was loved, accepted and embraced. All fear was gone and with it the shame and stigma she had carried for twelve long, painful and lonely years. At last she was truly clean!

Slowly, Miriam stood up, a new woman made whole.

Based on Mark 5

By faith, the power of God can be released to bring physical healing to the body. But it is only through a Love encounter, that the inner healing of a person's heart, emotions, or spirit can fully take place.

It takes us less than thirty seconds to read this encounter in Mark's gospel, but for the precious lady it was twelve years. Twelve long and painful years of her life. We don't know if she had been married, had children, or was single, but either way she would have been lonely. Cut off from any physically contact with friends or family while carrying the hurt of a life lost and dreams dashed, besides all the physical pain of her condition.

Discovering true identity...

If someone was unclean by law they had to live separately and would have to call out to anyone who was approaching them warning them that they were unclean and then step off the road. So that the clean person didn't have to get too near to them and risk becoming unclean too.

Imagine doing this for twelve years, constantly saying "I'm unclean". Indeed, in a society where only the clean were accepted. This would have compounded the sense of being second class, rejected and totally unacceptable. Being "unclean" would have become more than a description of her physical state, or her position in society. Much more profoundly it would have become part of her identity, what she fundamentally believed about who she was.

You may not be in that place, but what is your story? Is there something that you keep saying to other people, or yourself, to explain or justify why you are like you are?

Perhaps take a few minutes and listen to God... What truth is Father whispering to you about it?

What could you do to start declaring His truth instead?

Pressing in and overcoming...

With the Samaritan woman (John 4) God set it up as a one-to-one. I bet this woman would have loved that! A nice safe, discreet and private encounter with Jesus. Yet out here in the open, as an unclean woman, she had to break the Law of Moses and press in through a crowd of potentially hostile people, who might turn on her and stone her, in order to reach Jesus before she could be healed.

This lady was wanting physical healing for the problems in her physical body. But God's heart was for all of her being to be made whole. Maybe the very act of having to press in through the crowd for physical healing, was what helped to position her heart to be able to receive a far deeper inner healing? Healing of the emotional and psychological scars was just as important to God as the physical healing.

Perhaps you need healing in one area, but what does this story help you see about God's heart for every part of you?

Has your heart been stirred to hope for breakthrough by something God has said, but then the facts of your condition or circumstances have started to make you question it?

Truth is what God says, and it always triumphs over the facts! Facts are simply accurate statements about reality based on our experience, scientific understanding, feelings and even prejudices.

What was the last thing God said to you regarding this issue that bought you peace?

This truth that God has spoken is your anchor point, your resting place. The place to trust and hope from. Return to this truth and ask God to now show you the next step. For this solid anchor will protect you from the storms of life.

A Prayer of Blessing...

In Jesus name I bless you to know Father God's heart for you; to be healed, restored, and be made whole. I bless you to know that every part of your spirit, soul and body, your mind, will and emotions are all equally important to Him.

I bless you to release hopelessness and take hold of a fresh hope today in His loving presence. I bless you with the courage to press in, past any hurt or disappointments. To go beyond the limited expectations of others or yourself. To pursue and receive the fullness of all He desires for you.

I bless you to know that you are worth it. That Jesus died for you and paid the price for you to be restored and made whole in every way, simply because He loves you, adores you, treasures you and truly delights to be with you.

I bless you to know that not only have you been forgiven, but that you have also been made, and are now, completely clean. You are totally accepted and have been made right before Him.

I bless you with joy to rise above the expectations and constraints of other peoples' beliefs. To see beyond your current circumstances and facts, to the wonderful truth of the hope and future you have in God.

I bless you to arise and stand, face to face with your loving heavenly Father and enveloped in His loving embrace, as you journey together.

Alive again!

The night had been long. He was so tired, yet he could not sleep, not now. The fever had not broken as hoped. Indeed, it was burning her up even more and nothing could bring it down. It was not going to be long now... All he could do was to hold her damp limp hand in his, and with every faint breath his heart broke painfully inside.

"There's some boats arriving and Jesus of Nazareth is in one!" Someone shouted from outside.

Jairus knew all the stories about this controversial Rabbi from Nazareth. Indeed, he'd often heard him speak at the synagogue since the man had moved to Capernaum and talked to him on numerous occasions. The miracles and deliverances the man did were truly astonishing.

But he had also been involved with the heated debates with the other synagogue leaders in the area. He knew only one blessed by God could be doing all these miracles, indeed miracles that the Messiah was expected to do. Yet the Rabbi was not overthrowing the hated Roman occupation and bringing about Israel's deliverance as the scriptures clearly said the Messiah would do. Instead he was actually denouncing the religious leaders. The very people God had appointed to lead his people!

His theological questions would have to wait. The simple truth was that Jesus could heal. Getting up he left to go to Jesus. He didn't care if it would cost him his position in the synagogue. His daughter was dying and he would do anything for her. It did not take him long to run down to the shore. A large crowd had already gathered round the Rabbi but Jairus ploughed straight through it.

Grabbing hold of Jesus, he knelt before him, pleading. "Rabbi! My precious little girl is dying. Please will you come and put your hands on her. Unless you do there is no hope, Rabbi you are our only hope, please will you come at once, so that she will live? She's only twelve years old, far too young to die! She needs you!"

Nodding Jesus lifted him up and turned to go. With the press of the crowds around them they moved slowly back up the road. Much too slow for Jairus's liking. Suddenly the Rabbi stopped and turned back.

"Who touched me?"

What?! Jairus spun round looking wildly about, trying to see what had just happened to cause this delay. There was nothing going on!

"Who touched me?"

Whoever it was had better own up quickly, he thought. Time was running out. His daughter was dying!

"Who touched me?"

"Master there's a crowd pressing around us? Why are you asking who touched you?"

"Who touched me?"

Then that unclean woman stepped forward. What was she doing down here in the middle of this crowd! Falling at the Rabbi's feet she confessed that she had touched him.

What! Righteous anger and indignation rose up within him, warring with frustration and impatience. He did not need this delay; his daughter was dying!

Bending down Jesus touched her and gently lifted her head. "Daughter, your faith has healed you. Go in peace."

Slowly she stood up. The change was remarkable; it was like she became over ten years younger! He had forgotten just how beautiful Miriam had been, and indeed was again! She stood up straight, her face radiant and smiling.

He felt a tug at his sleeve and turning saw his servant. His heart went cold as fear gripped it. Everything stopped and he closed his eyes. He did not need to hear the message to know, he saw it in the servant's eyes. She was dead. His precious, beloved daughter was dead. All because of this stupid delay. He didn't begrudge Miriam being healed but there had not been enough time for both of them. Why couldn't she have waited? A few extra minutes would have been nothing to her after waiting twelve years. Now it was too late for his daughter!

"Don't be afraid" Jesus said "just believe".

The words were a point of light in the chaos of his emotions and pain, an anchor point. Opening his eyes, he looked at the Rabbi into those calm, undisturbed steady eyes. Taking a deep breath, he nodded. He didn't trust his voice, so remained silent. May be there was still hope. The transformation he had just witnessed of Miriam was truly miraculous.

Letting three of his disciples come with them, Jesus told the rest of his disciples to keep the crowds back. Then turning Jesus lead the way to Jairus's house. Jairus followed. He would say nothing, he would trust this Jesus of Nazareth, he would believe.

While they walked he thought about the stories of Jesus. Particularly about him raising the dead son of a widow at Nain. He had been sceptical about that when he first heard about it, but there had been many respectable witnesses present. If he did it once, then surely it could be done again? After all the prophet Daniel had prophesied that the Messiah would raise the dead. So maybe…?

When they arrived back at the house the mourners were already gathering and wailing a death song. He felt his heart being tugged and a lump rise in his throat.

No! he would believe!

Entering the house Jesus asked the mourners, "Why all this commotion and wailing? The child is not dead, only asleep."

The scorn that they directed at Jesus shocked Jairus. The grief they had been displaying so dramatically seconds before was gone in an instance as they laughed at him. Clearly their grief was a shallow façade. He felt disgusted with them for intruding in his pain.

"Out!"

Jairus felt the hair stand up on the back of his neck. The command was not shouted, yet it carried throughout the house. Spoken such authority, that one word, that everyone instantly left and only his wife remained. With red stained eyes, she walked numbly towards him. He held her silently. He knew her grief, it mirrored his.

Entering the bedroom, Jairus again felt the grip of fear in his heart mingled with searing pain as he saw his daughter lying there. There was no doubt now that she was truly dead. It was too late. Best face the facts with dignity and let Jesus go...

No! he would believe!

Jesus walked over to his daughter, bent down and taking hold of her hand said. "Little girl, I am telling you to get up."

The words were gently spoken, yet the power and authority with which they were spoken rocked Jairus to the core. These were not just words spoken by a man. There was divine power and authority. He could feel it in the air. He felt small and vulnerable, indeed terrified. Yet also exhilarated and so alive.

Instantly the colour returned to his daughters face and he heard the soft whisper as she drew in a deep breath, just as when she was peacefully asleep. Then she opened her eyes and sat up. She sat up! Alive! ALIVE!

His daughter was alive! The tears ran down his face, HIS DAUGHTER WAS ALIVE!

As her face lit up with the most radiant smile, joy surged throughout his whole body. His daughter was dead but now she was alive again!!!! She got up and walked over towards him. He just held her. There were no words... He just held his beautiful daughter so full of life once again!

She was alive!!!!

"Get her something to eat", Jesus said.

His wife quickly grabbed some food from the side and they watched as she ate it. Such joy and delight seeing her heathy appetite again. He felt his heart would burst. He wanted to shout it out from the roof top! She was alive again!

"Do not tell anyone about what has just happened here."

Shocked, Jairus looked at Jesus. Why not he thought? This was the most amazing miracle ever; he couldn't keep it to himself! Besides, raising the dead was strong evidence that Jesus was the Messiah so why not declare it? After all, what better way to help to further his cause?

It just didn't make sense. Jesus consistently did so many miracles that provided strong evidence that he was the Messiah. Yet in many other ways he was behaving very differently to the conquering king the scriptures clearly said the Messiah would be. It just didn't make sense.

What he did know though was this, his daughter was dead and now she was alive. Only God could have done that. Only God. Thankfulness and worship poured from his heart... Only God.

Based on Mark 5:22-34

Willingness to trust...

It is very easy for us to have our pre-conceived ideas about how God should behave or what He should do. However, wisdom is found in embracing what God is doing and not to take offense at what we perceive He isn't doing.

That may be a huge or even new thing to embrace, but if it is... consider it, after all isn't He God?

Perhaps, press pause on your many questions and feelings and begin by thanking God for all you do see Him doing and for all He has shown himself to be to you?

Finding the way forward...

God is sovereign and all powerful, He can do all things. However, not all the events and circumstances of our lives are what He desires or are of His making. For He has given us, all of us, freewill to make our own choices, as love can only be expressed through a freewill choice. That's why God respects our choices, even the ones that grieve Him for the harm they cause to us or others, whether those consequences happen immediately or take generations to become known.

However, if we are willing, regardless of what has happened through our choices or the choices of others, He can always make a way. Bringing redemption and leading us on a path that by His grace we can walk, to come into a place of breakthrough, wholeness and peace.

Is there an area where you are still waiting for a breakthrough?

Why not thank Him that He holds this in His hands and let praise and worship rise out of your heart as you trust in His goodness. God is able to handle your toughest questions and your loudest cries...

Perhaps your breakthrough will begin to be found right in the midst of those moments as you allow Him to come close and you choose to connect with Him and be real in the pain?

A Prayer of Blessing…

In the name of Jesus, I bless you with peace that comes from experiencing and knowing the goodness of God. That comes regardless of the things you've journeyed through or your present circumstances. That comes from knowing your heavenly Father always is utterly trustworthy.

I bless you with grace to stay focused on what God has said to you and not be swayed by the emotions or arguments of those around you.

I bless you with knowing the value of God's word to you, of His faithfulness to fulfil all His promises. I bless you with courage to draw strength from Him as you co labour and partner with Him, and so fulfil your potential. I bless you to be real, vulnerable, truly honest and to press towards Him in your struggles and pain.

I bless you to believe in His goodness, His power, and His unfailing love and I bless you to keep your eyes on the unswerving calm eyes of Jesus knowing He is able.

Come!

The waves were racing towards him and crashing wildly as Peter stood bracing his legs in the stern of the boat. He was in his element here, the captain and master of the sea! He loved the sea, it's different moods. Even in the storms, though there was danger, he knew what he was doing pitting his wits against the elements. He knew how to read the wind and waves and keep the boat pointing safely in the right direction. It was exhilarating. He felt so alive!

The storm was strong but he'd weathered worse. He knew how far the boat could safely lean, some of the others were not so sure. He smiled as they gripped the sides looking anxiously around. It was so tempting to let the boat lean a bit more so that the water splashed over the side onto them. It was OK though as he was in control.

Suddenly Mathew cried out and pointed to the side, Peter turned to look. He squinted to make out a shape moving between the crashing waves, an apparition out there on the water! A figure could clearly be seen walking on the water, parallel to the boat looking as if it was intending to head past them.

"What is it?"

"It must be a ghost!"

"What do we do?"

The exhilarating fear of the storm was swiftly replaced with a more uncontrollable fear, a fear of the unknown, something supernatural and dangerous. Peter shivered and it had nothing to do with the cold rain, all his bold confidence had washed away and had been replaced by a timidity, an uncertainty, like a huge wave crashing over him.

"Do not be afraid, it is I."

Jesus? The voice sounded like Jesus's and now he looked again, it looked like him too. But they had left him on the other side of the lake! What was he doing out here and how was he walking on the water? The thought of Jesus awakened his boldness again. Peter knew that if Jesus did something, then sooner or later he would ask them to do it. He loved his Master and would follow him anywhere, even to walking on the water.

He didn't even stop to think, he just shouted. "Jesus, if that's you then tell me to come on the water!".

"Come…"

Peter shivered again, but this time with a thrill as joy leapt in his heart joining with his boldness. Yes, he had heard that voice and command before, when Jesus called him to be a follower and fisher of men. Without a second thought he let go of the rudder leaving the boat to flounder in the rocking sea. He just swung his legs over the side, and climbed out of the boat and stepped onto the crashing waves.

"Peter! What do you think you are doing?" screamed Thomas. But all Peter saw was the joy and pride in Jesus's eyes as he looked straight at his Master and walked towards him, on the water! Wow this was amazing; he was walking on the water towards his Master.

The wind whipped his hair around his face and the spray stung his eyes. He turned his head up wind for a moment, to brush the clinging hair away. I'm walking on water the thought, it's unreal! Looking up he watched the rolling waves crashing around him. Instinctively spotting the biggest wave approaching, he braced himself for the impact, as it crashed and the spray stung his eyes yet again.

This was madness he thought. He was too exposed and getting wet, soaking wet. He was wading knee deep in water! I'm sinking! "Help!" he cried turning back to Jesus and reaching out as he slid chest deep into the cold water. Exhilaration now replaced with sheer terror!

Immediately Peter felt his hand being gripped in a strong embrace as Jesus grabbed him. Lifting him up again onto the water. The fear that had been so real moments before was gone, washed away with a wave of love as Peter held Jesus's hand and was lifted up, to stand once again on the water, face to face with his master. The storm still raged around them but all Peter could see was the joy and pride in his master's face, as he gently said.

"How briefly you trusted me. Why did you stop?"

Together they walked to the boat and climbed inside. As they continued on Peter pondered on what had just happened. He had just walked on the water but why had he been so quick to turn away? He knew why and was so sorry for letting his master down. He had taken his eyes off Jesus for just an instance, and instead relied on his own knowledge and experience as a fisherman to tell him the truth about what was happening. He would never do that again he promised himself. From now on he would always trust his Master, that he loved so much. He would always follow him, no matter what.

Based on Mt 14, Mk 6, Jn 6

Called...

Don't you just love Peter. So often he comes across as super confident, speaking or acting before thinking, jumping in with both feet. But Jesus never said to him you must wait until you are ready... or are good enough... or smart enough... Rather Jesus simply said "come", and then took Peter on a journey of life through which he grew and changed into the man of God he was created to be.

Growing Faith...

Several times Jesus talked about the disciples having little faith. The word that is translated little can equally be translated as brief, as in a little or brief amount of time. We are always exercising faith, always making a choice to trust something or someone: The chair will take my weight... The other cars will stop at the red lights...

Have you ever watched a child learning to ride a bike? They manage for a brief moment before wobbling and falling to the side. As a father with my own son, I was over-joyed for that brief moment. But then through encouragement, as he practiced and stayed focused, there came a point when the brief moments became longer moments until finally becoming a lasting moment. He had caught his balance and was riding the bike!

ENCOUNTERS

We can feel discouraged with our 'brief moments of faith' but Daddy God wants to celebrate those brief moments with you. Listen to him and let him tell you how proud he is of you, and receive his encouragement.

What are you trusting God for right now?

What are you trusting God IN right now?

How is your faith being expressed?

Knowing you are loved...

In the gospels Peter comes across as being confident and zealous in his love for Jesus. In contrast however, John is confident that he is loved by Jesus. I think it's telling then that though all the disciples deserted Jesus in the garden, the only disciple with the courage to come back and be at the foot of the cross was the one who truly knew he was loved by Jesus.

Perhaps it has seemed most important to tell God that you love Him, but how much do you know that He truly loves you? Spend some time meditating on the times He has shown you his love.

What memory comes to mind when you think of God showing you He loves you?

How did that memory help you experience God's love for you?

ENCOUNTERS

It is in the place of knowing we are loved where trust grows... perhaps meditate on some love experiences you have had with God.

A prayer of Blessing...

In Jesus name I bless you to know that you are loved! That being loved has nothing to do with your performance, actions or ability. I bless you to know that Father loves you simply because He does! It is who He is, Love. He always has and He always will love you. You are His most precious and treasured child.

I bless you with the courage and confidence that comes from knowing you are fully loved and accepted. I bless you with freedom to step out and experiment. To be bold and take a risk, knowing whatever happens you are held in the palm of His hands. That He has your back covered and will journey with you.

I bless you to know that failing doesn't make you a failure, it simply means you learnt and that there is a new way forward. I bless you with freedom from the fear of failure as you know it doesn't define who you are.

I bless you with being filled with the joy that comes from having done something new, from stepping out and taking a risk. I bless you with the joy that comes from experiencing your Father's faithfulness and provision in a way you've not done before. I bless you to enjoy the journey and adventure of life, discovering who He made you to be.

The Best Party, Ever!

The fighting had been fierce and relentless, only the bravest would be able to survive. But the enemy was just too strong, they were about to be overwhelmed. Then suddenly David came running up and swung his sword as the Spirit of God came on him like he did on Samson of old and he pushed back the Philistines. They were going to win…

"Ouch! Careful with that stick Eldad!".

"Sorry Michael"

The two boys paused their heroic battle and ran to catch-up with their friends again as they headed on to Bethsaida.

Eldad loved acting out stories almost as much as he loved listening to them. Any stories, but the best were of how God had set His people free long ago. When God used to talk to the prophets and do amazing miracles. He so wished that he could have been there to see and experience them for himself.

David and Goliath was his favourite. David had been just a young shepherd boy and yet because he trusted in God he was able to fight the lions and bears, and then giants. He smiled to himself how he used to boast to his mum that he too would kill lions and bears and giants with his sling when he was bigger. His mum would laugh and say; "of course you will Eldad." Then she'd pick him up, hug him and kiss him with her eyes shining.

He was older now though, but he still believed that he would be a hero, someone special. That he was born to be and do amazing things.

It was yesterday afternoon when they heard that the Rabbi Jesus from Nazareth was staying over in Bethsaida for a few days. Eldad desperately wanted to go and listen to him. He had heard amazing stories from some traders about this new Rabbi, who not only told great stories but he also actually did miracles too!

"Mum, please can we go?" He'd ran and asked her as soon as he had heard.

"I'm sorry Eldad but we can't take you. I have to stay as Berenice is going to have the baby any day now and your Father has to see the blacksmith whilst he is visiting the village".

"But mum, I could go on my own! I'm a big boy now and it's not that far to Bethsaida. I could easily run there and back without stopping and I know the way, and I would be out of your way too, and you say that I should learn all I can, and the other children are going, and you promised that when I was bigger I'd be allowed to go to Bethsaida on my own, and I am bigger now!" he pleaded.

"I will talk with your father when he comes home this evening and we will see what he says", his mother smiled. "Now go and help your brother gather some more firewood, we're getting low again".

He had been on the edge of his seat all evening, whilst his father decided if he was to be allowed to go on his own and listen to the Rabbi. Eldad knew better than to badger his father so he waited as patiently as he could, nibbling half-heartedly at his food. Finally, after the evening meal was finished his father turned to him and said yes, but that he must stay with the other older children from the village.

His heart leapt with joy, he was going to get to hear and see the Rabbi! That night he was so excited to be allowed to go that he lay awake for a long time thinking about all he had heard about Rabbi Jesus. He was known for telling wonderful stories but more amazingly he actually did real miracles! Lots of people had been healed and set free from demons. Eldad really hoped that he would get to see a miracle too. Maybe a leg growing back again…

At first light Eldad was up and ready to go, but mum had insisted he wait while she got some food ready for him. "You will be glad enough to have this food later," she laughed. After what seemed like forever she handed him a bag, kissed him and off he ran to join the other children.

As they approached Bethsaida, they saw a large crowd up on the hillside. That had to be where the Rabbi was, so off the children ran. The Rabbi was already talking to the crowd when they arrived. Eldad had never seen so many people, but being small meant that he was able to easily get through the crowds. Finding a spot to one side of the rock where Jesus was sitting, he settled down to listen.

The Rabbi talked about many things. What God was like and the things that God had done. Often he would just tell stories. There were so many stories, some were similar to ones he had heard before, but many others were new. Eldad didn't really know what most of the stories meant but they fired his imagination and he loved them! He loved the sound of the Rabbi's voice. He could tell that the Rabbi was good at imagining many wonderful things.

One story was about a farmer sowing seed in different soils. The grown-ups all seemed puzzled by it, but if he became a farmer when he grew up then he knew that he would always sow the seed on the good ground and have big harvests.

Another story was about lighting lamps on the hills. He imagined building the biggest pole ever and lighting a lamp so bright on top of it so that everyone would see the light and know where to go safely. Even old uncle Ben, who always complained it was getting dark, would be able to see by it.

It was late in the day when the Rabbi finally stopped talking. His disciples were asking him to send everyone away so they could get something to eat. Suddenly Eldad realised how hungry he was. He had been so engrossed with listening that he had completely forgotten to eat his lunch! Picking up the bag he started to open it, he was ravenous. Mum was right as usual he thought with a smile, he was glad to have the food now! She was so good to him and had given him a generous portion.

"You give them something to eat," the Rabbi said to his disciples.

Eldad watched as they looked around, clearly they had no food with them. Eldad looked down at his lunch as his tummy rumbled. Suddenly it didn't look that big. He was a big boy now and needed to eat properly, if he shared it even with one other person then he would go hungry. But as he looked at the loaves and fish he remembered what the Rabbi had said about loving others. It had been easy to agree when the Rabbi was talking, but now he had a chance to show what love looked like. Though he would go hungry he wanted to live like the Rabbi said, so gathering the food back up he went over to the men.

"I've got some food the Rabbi can have," Eldad pipped up. One of the disciples, called Andrew, turned and smiled and took him to the Rabbi.

"Thank you," the Rabbi said as Eldad handed him the food. Then turning to his disciples the Rabbi told them to get the people to sit down in groups of fifty or a hundred. It took quite a while before everybody was sorted as there was so many of them. Eldad watched the Rabbi, wondering what he was going to do next. Deep down there was a feeling of excitement in his tummy. He was hungry but he just knew something good was going to happen, something wonderful!

Then the Rabbi lifted up the food and simply said thank you to God, broke the food up and handed the pieces to the disciples.

Eldad gasped. The broken pieces grew bigger as the Rabbi gave them to the disciples! Rubbing his eyes, Eldad looked again to make sure. Yes, there were twelve men each holding a full loaf of bread in their hands! With great big grins they turned to go to the nearest groups of people. Each one carrying a loaf of bread and a fish.

Eldad decided to follow the disciple Andrew. Every time the disciple broke a piece of bread or fish and handed it to someone it just grew bigger! Right there in their hands! Eldad took a piece as Andrew handed it to him and looked at it. It just looked like an ordinary piece of bread. In fact, just like the ones his mother made with the twisty bit at the end that went crunchy like he liked. He broke it himself into two pieces and nothing happened. Just two smaller pieces, but then as he handed one of the piece to a boy next to him, that piece grew! Looking down at his own piece, that too had grown bigger!

Laughing he broke his piece again. Again nothing happened until he gave one away. It was happening all over the place. People were laughing as they broke the bread and gave it away. This was the most fun Eldad had ever had! People were smiling and laughing and crying and so happy! There was more food here than he had ever seen in his life. Was this what it was like when God sent the manna in the wilderness he wondered?

Wandering back to his little spot near the Rabbi, Eldad thought how wonderful it was to give something away. His mum would be so amazed! He was so glad now that she had insisted that he wait while she got his lunch ready!!! No way could she have known what was going to happen, yet her simple act of love for him, provided the food for the miracle of feeding this huge crowd.

He was so filled with joy, not only did he get to see a miracle, but even more amazingly, he got to be part of the miracle! Just by giving away what little he had to the Rabbi Jesus. It was so simple, so beautiful he thought. Looking up he saw the Rabbi watching him. The Rabbi smiled and gave him a wink. Eldad smiled back and felt his heart overwhelm with love as he suddenly realised that God had given him the opportunity to partner with Him.

Based on John 6

Partnering with God...

God wants us to partner with him. In John 15:15 Jesus says that we are no longer servants but friends. A servant is told what to do, but a friend is involved in and influences the decision making processes.

The fact that He no longer called them servants, meant that at one point He did. Friendship is built on servanthood, as in a healthy relationship we each value and look to serve one-another.

As friends sometimes we might do what I want, and at other times we would do what you want. It's the same with God. King David wanted to build God a temple. God's response basically was... "Heaven is my throne and earth is my footstool, I don't need a temple. However, I love your heart and that it's what you want to do, so let's do it like this..."

Is there something that's been burning in your heart that you are wondering if God is inviting you to partner with Him on it?

Why not share your thoughts and feelings with Him, and as you listen to His thoughts and feelings, see where He takes you?

To us or through us...

Scripture dose not say exactly how the food got multiplied. It could be that suddenly there was food appearing everywhere like the mana appeared in the wilderness. However, we're told that afterwards the crowds wanted to make him king by force, so this miracle must have had a much greater impact on them than the many other miracles they had already seen him do.

Personally, I believe that in this miracle everyone was involved at some point. As it's one thing to observe a miracle but totally different having the miracle performed through you. Imagine it, there's great expectation that Jesus is the Messiah because of all the miracles He is doing. Now thousands of us have all experienced the power of God flowing through us. God is with us and nothing is impossible! It has to be the right time for our deliverance from Roman oppression and becoming a world super power again. Let's do it! Let's make him King!

Is there a breakthrough that God seems silent on?

Why not ask Him if He's waiting for you to release something to start the process of the miracle?

Prayer of Blessing...

In the name of Jesus, I bless you to know the intimacy of friendship with God. That as His friend you are free to discover and express your heart's desires with Him and in so doing you bring pleasure to His heart.

I bless you with the joy of partnering with Him. Of knowing how much He values your thoughts and feelings. I bless you to dream with Him, talking and exploring together the many potential paths there are for your life's journey in discovering your identity.

I bless you with the courage to give what you have by faith trusting Him with what He can do with it. That you will step forward with boldness into the opportunities to partner with Him.

I bless you in the silent moments before the breakthrough, to be filled with an outrageous hope. That joyful expectation in the goodness of God. To be steadfastly confident in His utter faithfulness to lead you.

The Light

It had not been a good start to the day. Someone had moved his official begging blanket from where he had put it down and it had taken quite some time to find it. By rights it gave him a prime position at the gates to Jericho, but without it he was not allowed to beg there. Angry and frustrated he arrived late only to discover that the best spot in the gate itself was already taken. So here he was stuck to one side of the road in a lesser position where fewer people were passing.

He felt so discouraged, though he was fortunate to be allowed to beg at the gate. The harshness of each day wearied him on the inside till he felt empty. Not only had he lost his sight, but his life had been robbed from him too.

For some reason there had not been as many people passing through the gate, or at least not on the side of the road he had chosen to sit. Even those few that did were not as generous as usual, and now he could feel the full heat of the sun on his face as it moved across the sky as he was no longer in the shade of the city walls. Now the terrible choice... should he move and find some shelter and gain relief, or endure the heat in the hope that someone would take pity on him and give him something?

How he longed to see again, to be free from this dark prison and be done with this beggar's life. Though it had been years he still pictured in his mind some precious faces. Their faces would look different now, he could feel the wrinkles in their skin when he touched them. Images of the red and golden colours of a sunrise. Dappled light dancing on the underside of the leaves of the trees as it was reflected from the river. But it would only be by a miracle from God that he would ever be able to see again. Not only had darkness covered his eyes, but his heart too.

He had heard of the miracle working Rabbi, Jesus of Nazareth. Some people said that he was the Messiah, the son of David, others said that he couldn't be because he was a bastard, born out of wedlock. Though it was obvious to Bartimaeus that anyone so blessed and favoured by God in doing all those miracles clearly had to be the Messiah. None of the prophets of old had done anywhere as many miracles. But he had no way of traveling to find Jesus.

Bartimaeus was suddenly roused from his deep ponderings by the sound of a crowd in the city heading towards the gates. He wondered what it could be as there were no religious festivals or anything else going on that day. They did sound happy though which was good, as happy people were usually more generous.

"Alms for a blind man," he cried wearily shaking the bowl.

"Thank you Sir. What's going on?" he asked as a few coins were dropped into his bowl by someone.

"Its Jesus of Nazareth! He's coming through the town and heading up to Jerusalem."

What? Jesus of Nazareth! Jesus is here? Out of the depths of his heart a glimmer of hope rose up. At last it was his chance to be healed. But he couldn't tell where Jesus was or which direction he would take on leaving the city. Though he would have to pass reasonably close by. So he shouted out as loud as he could. "Son of David, have mercy on me!"

"Be quiet you!" Those gathering in front of him began to harshly rebuke him, roughly jostling around him.

Sitting behind a crowd he would never be noticed, so shouting louder again and again he called out in his crackled voice. "Son of David, have mercy on me!". He did not care what those around said. He had to make sure Jesus heard him. Today, he would see again!

Suddenly the tone of the voices around him changed, they were no longer aggressive. They began to part and make space for him. "Have courage! He's asking for you. Here, take my hand, he's this way."

As courage and strength arose inside of him, Bartimaeus got up and deliberately threw his begging blanket down. He would not be needing that again! He was going to see! Reaching out his hands tentatively then more confidently, to those in front of him he stepped into the crowd which slowly parted and guided him, hand by hand, through to where Jesus waited.

Sensing an open space in front of him, he reached out with shaking hands, and someone else took hold of his hands. They were rough hands, a worker's hands, they held him firmly. The calm clear voice asked "What do you want me to do for you?" This must be Jesus he thought. His whole body shook with the vulnerability and the anticipation of this moment.

"Rabbi, let me see again."

"Go, your faith has healed you."

Immediately there was a burst of light. Was it just inside of him, or was it really real? Bartimaeus blinked a few times. It was real! for the first time in a long, long while he saw a few blurred shapes and muted colours. It took a moment to make sense of it as a kaleidoscope of bright colours and detail shapes flood his mind. Gasping and panting, as joy overwhelmed him he looked around drinking everything in. And there standing in front of him was a man, laughing at him so full of joy!

As more face crowded in front of him and people shouted. "Look at his eyes, they are clear! He can see!"

Looking further away he saw the trees, the city walls, the mountains and the light, and way above the blue, glorious azure blue sky! He could see again! PRAISE GOD he could see again!!

Blinking away huge tears of joy he turned back to thank Jesus, but Jesus had already headed off again down the road. Bartimaeus followed. Wherever Jesus went he would now go. It didn't matter where. The Messiah had given him back his sight again and he would give him everything, from now on his life belonged to the Messiah.

Based on Mk 10

Resting Faith…

When Jesus healed someone he would often say to them, "Your faith has…" or "According to your faith…". So we tend to look at the level of confidence we have in the outcome as a measure of faith, and the more difficult the problem to be overcome the greater a measure of faith is required. So we think of Bartimaeus as showing great faith in that he threw away his livelihood before he was healed because of he was super-confidence that Jesus would heal him.

Whilst I believe it is true there's a connection between faith and healing. All who came to Jesus were healed, regardless of the level of confidence or faith they expressed. The simple fact of coming to Jesus was a step of faith. That was enough for Jesus to respond to and completely and instantly heal them, irrespective of the mix of confidence and doubt they had.

Perhaps, that is something you haven't really thought before. Ponder what you just read... Jesus healed people irrespective of the mix of confidence and doubt they had.

Instead of trying to be, or feel more confident, why not rest in the simple truth that God is able and willing, and in that safe place be vulnerable and share your hearts desires and leave the rest to Him...

Action Faith...

We believe in God – that he is who he says he is. We place our hope in his promises – that he will do what he says he will do. Faith then is stepping out and taking a risk where we become dependent on the truth that he is who he says he is, and he will do what he says he will do. Faith demonstrates trust, as it is trust expressed in an action, and it is through relationship that we grow in trust.

Like the woman healed from the issue of blood, Bartimaeus had to overcome some of the circumstances around him.

Are you waiting for a breakthrough, sensing that now's the time, that Jesus is near but nothing is happening? Why not ask Him what simple step of trust you need to take?

Prayer of Blessing...

In the name of Jesus, I bless you to know that you have Father's full and undivided attention. I bless you to know the anticipation He is feeling regarding your breakthrough and the passion with which He is ready and willing to respond with.

I bless you to know His love and be bold and confident in His goodness towards you. That He is actively and continually working on your behalf.

I bless you with courage to step out, to take a risk. Not to be put off by circumstances, or facts, or other people's opinions. I bless you with the vulnerability to be real and I bless you to know the joy of seeing His faithfulness to you yet again being manifest.

I bless you to grow in trust as you pursue intimacy and relationship with Him. Not for what you can get out of the relationship but simply because of love.

Unrestrained

O h how she loved him; more than a mother for her child, more than a lover. He was everything to her, as she sat and listened to him, she felt that her heart would burst. The joy and freedom he had bought her into, the words of wisdom and love that had so transformed her life. Restoring her dignity and giving hope for the future. Even raising her brother after he had been dead four days! With everything in her she knew that he was the Messiah. God's promise, the Anointed One, who would deliver them all.

Yet she could not throw off this feeling in the pit of her stomach, a premonition that something was about to change. She knew he sensed it too. Though he never seemed to change, there was a resolve and determination about him she'd not seen before. Recently he had often spoken about suffering but the others seemed oblivious to it. Always talking to each other about victory, a new order, and who was going to get to do what.

But while she too believed that would happen, she was sure there was something terrible that was going to happen first. Things were coming to a head with the authorities back in Jerusalem and she felt an uneasy apprehension. A storm was brewing and about to break. She had seen the way the leaders looked at him. They had always hated him and wanted him dead.

She shivered, feeling sick inside. What could she do to show her love for him, what gift to measure it with? How could she fully express her love and the gratitude of her heart to him for the healing and cleansing of her life? Then she remembered the jar of Nard. That was it! She would use it to anoint him and wash his feet. She would stoop to the lowliest of jobs to serve him with the greatest gift she had.

Quietly she got up and slipped out of the house. Running home, she went into the inner room and got the jar. It was her most prized possession. For years she had treasured it, keeping it hidden and safe for a special occasion. Now was the time to use it. How she loved its sweet fragrant aroma. Holding it close she carefully walked back to the house, remembering the many sacrifices that she had made to get it.

No one took any notice as she came quietly back into the room. No one noticed as she made her way behind Jesus whilst he continued to talk – not until she broke the seal and started to pour some of the nard onto his head, anointing him. The aroma quickly filled the room. Whatever it was that was going to happen, she would always trust and believe in him, her Messiah.

There were gasps of astonishment as she continued to pour out more and more of the nard, so that it ran down onto his clothes. Like the anointing oil of a prophet of old upon a king or high priest. The aroma now flooding not just the room, but the whole house, even spilling out into the courtyard and street outside. It caused people to stop, to turn and come to see what was happening.

Coming round in front of him she continued to pour out the nard all over his feet. Unrestrained and unashamed, like her love for her Messiah. His love and words had washed her clean, he had made her beautiful inside again. Now it was her turn, as she served him and washed his feet clean.

Angry voices intruded on her devotion; judging, condemning. She didn't care what they thought! She wept with sorrow, she wept with joy. With love and thankfulness, she gave it all. Holding nothing back, pouring the nard and her heart out as an offering to him, as she washed his feet and dried them with her hair. Her Messiah! She was forever his, he was forever hers.

Finally, as she sat back and looked up into his face, radiant with love, she released that she too had become covered with the nard. All over her own hands and hair, splashed onto her own clothes. Her love gift received by him yet covering her too. They were joined and whatever happened next they would face it as one.

Based on Mk 14 and Jn 12

Every person and situation is different and God will respond uniquely in each case. The adventure of an encounter is that each time it is unique, yet intensely personal. And just like a lover, Jesus delights to encounter us again and again, each time powerfully unique as we journey with him.

Worship without restraint...

To the outsider, abandoned worship can often look beyond extravagant, extreme and inappropriate. But to the one who is worshipping, it is the natural expression of a heart touched and overwhelmed by Love and the goodness of God.

With our words we give thanks for what God has done in the past, and we praise Him for what He will do in the future. But it is in worship where we stand face to face before Him, in the present moment. In worship He becomes everything.

What does abandoned worship look like for you? Or does unrestrained worship make you feel uncomfortable?

If so why not take this precious moment, for in this moment you get to bring your vulnerable heart open before Him, trusting in His love and goodness. Your worship doesn't have to look like anyone else's, just yours…

There are many languages of love, different ways to express our hearts and making an intimate connection. If you feel you are going through a dry season and that God feels distant to you, maybe He is wanting to reveal more of Himself to you in a new love language? In a new way?

Whatever moments you have, press in for more. Close your eyes and lay as if you're at His feet. Sing the feelings inside your heart, begin to draw or paint or just sit allowing His presence to fill the space, pouring over Him and you, uniting you as one.

A Prayer of Blessing…

In the name of Jesus, I bless you to know your Father God's love. That He is Love, and the One who always has and always will love you. I bless you to know this Love that surpasses anything you have experienced so far in your life journey of adventure with Him.

I bless you with the freedom to fully express your heart as a response in worship to God. To step beyond the man-made religious boundaries of decorum and decency. To connect heart to heart, spirit to spirit with Him, where He becomes everything to you, all-consuming.

I bless you to love, even as you have been loved. Without restraint, without condition. To give, not counting the cost. To pour out, withholding nothing. To risk it all, simply because He is worthy. Just as He did for you because you are worthy.

I bless you with fresh intimate encounters that are real, that are yours, that are true. I bless you with the peace of knowing that you are one with God, now and forever, and that nothing has, nor ever will, separate you from His Love.

The Cost

Bartholomew sat back and sipped the cool drink as the breeze gently blew in through the window. The celebrations had gone on late into the night and he was feeling a little delicate this morning. The gamble he had made, to finance sending the ships out earlier than usual, had paid off. It had been another very good business year, yet again he was blessed by God.

Yet not everything had gone well. Joshua, one of his best captains, had not survived. He'd caught a fever and died just days before reaching home. Life was so fragile even for those blessed by God. He was enjoying God's favour and blessing on his life now, but what of eternal life? How could he be sure that he'd done enough? He'd asked a number of the local Rabbis but they all re-iterated the same thing; obey the Law and give to the local synagogue.

He already did all that but there was still a constant niggling doubt that this was not sufficient to earn eternal life. In his heart he longed for greater assurance. Maybe the miracle working Rabbi, Jesus of Nazareth would be a good person to ask. Clearly this man walked closer to God than other men. He was supposed to be passing through sometime today, he would go and ask him.

As he headed down the road he could see a large crowd of people coming. This would be Jesus. First impressions were always important so he waited at the crossroads where he would be seen as

Jesus approached. Staying still he allowed the crowds to go round him until Jesus drew nearer.

Going up to the Rabbi he asked. "Good Rabbi, what must I do to inherit eternal life?"

"Why do you call me good? No one is good – except God alone. As for good works, you know the commandments: 'You shall not murder, you shall not commit adultery, you shall not steal, you shall not give false testimony, you shall not defraud, honour your father and mother.'"

Yes, yes, thought Bartholomew, that's the stock answer everyone quotes. I already do all that but still I know something is lacking, it simply can't be enough to earn eternal life. He prided himself on being a good judge of character. He could see the love in the Rabbi's eyes, and felt humbled. Here indeed was a good man of God who would be able to really answer his question, who would be able to give him the truth if he pursued it.

"Rabbi, I've kept all these since I was a boy, but what else is necessary?"

For a moment the Rabbi paused as he looked at him, then said. "One thing you lack. Go, sell everything you have and give to the poor, and you will have treasure in heaven. Then come, follow me."

What?! Sell everything? Give away the blessings that God had given him because of his faithfulness and obedience to the law? The very evidence of God's favour on his life? That's totally ridiculous! Crazy! How would he survive? He would become totally dependent on others, just like a common beggar! He can't be serious.

Bartholomew looked at Jesus to be sure he had heard right. There was love and compassion in Jesus' eyes, but no yielding. The truth had been asked for and given, and now had to either be accepted and embraced, or rejected.

Bartholomew turned away with a heavy heart. He could not make this decision lightly. He had been so confident in what he had achieved and his ability to keep the Law. Yet the words of this Rabbi rang true in his heart. He needed to think. He longed for assurance but could he afford to pay the price? To give up all the treasures in this life for treasures in eternal life?

Could he become so totally surrendered to God, trusting in him alone and not rely on his own strength, wealth or ability? That was the crux, he realised. Assurance would only come through surrender and trust, when one was in an intimate relationship with God, the one who gives eternal life.

He did want the assurance, but he also enjoyed the security and pleasures that came with the wealth he had worked so hard for. And the respect and influence it gave him with the Romans and religious leaders. What was he to do…?

As he walked slowly home he looked over at a beggar at the side of the road, and pondered for a long time. Either one of them could be dead the next day. So were they really that different anyway before God?

Based on Mt 19, Mk 10, and Lk 18

Assurance through surrender…

The desire and need for assurance is strong within us. But we are used to living in a world where assurance is based on what we have, or on what we have been able to do or achieve to get it. However, our salvation and eternal life can never be earned. It is not based on us at all but can only come when we surrender totally to God and trust in Him alone. In trusting that what Jesus did by his life, death and resurrection, is more than sufficient.

Do you know, beyond any doubt, that you are saved and forever held in Father God's loving arms?

John 1:12 NET *"But to all who have received him – those who believe in his name – he has given the right to become God's children."*

John 5:24 NET *"I tell you the solemn truth, the one who hears my message and believes the one who sent me has eternal life and will not be condemned, but has crossed over from death to life."*

Acts 4:12 NET *"And there is salvation in no one else, for there is no other name under heaven given among people by which we must be saved."*

Ephesians 2:8-9 NET *"For by grace you are saved through faith, and this is not from yourselves, it is the gift of God; it is not from works, so that no one can boast."*

Titus 3:4-7 NET But *"when the kindness of God our Savior and his love for mankind appeared, he saved us not by works of righteousness that we have done but on the basis* *of his mercy, through the washing of the new birth and the renewing of the Holy Spirit, whom he poured out on us in full measure through Jesus Christ our Savior. And so, since we have been justified by his grace, we become heirs with the confident expectation of eternal life. "*

Acceptance before understanding...

One of the most profound things God has ever said to me was. "Acceptance comes before understanding. If you will accept what I say before you understand it, then I can do more in you and more through you."

It is so easy to limit God to what we understand. But in truth there is so much more to discover. It is by journeying through the mystery of the unknown of God, that we discover more of who He is.

Is there something God has spoken to you that you don't understand?

What might a simple act of acceptance look like?

Surrendering a promise or treasure...

God promises us that He is our exceedingly great reward (Gen 15:1). He gave this promise to Abraham, along with the promise that He would have a son. Isaac was his greatest treasure but then God asked him to lay it down. Perhaps God is speaking to you to lay down a treasure or a dream, perhaps one you have held close to your heart your whole life? Perhaps like Abraham He will give it you back? Perhaps He has a better plan? Perhaps you need to let it go whatever happens.

If that's hard, why?

Is God bringing you back to treasuring Him most of all?

Prayer of Blessing...

In the name of Jesus, I bless you to trust solely in the goodness of God. That out of love alone Father chose you, paid the price for you and has invited you into an eternal intimate relationship with Himself.

I bless you to know the peace that goes beyond all understanding. To have the assurance that you are safe in His arms and can fully surrender all that you are to Him. Even as He has already fully surrendered all that He is for you.

I bless you with the courage to lay down those things that you hold as treasures and trusting in the greatest treasure of all. I bless you to enjoy the wonder and mystery of God as you allow Him to be your greatest treasure. To be constantly blown away with the extravagant breadth and depth of His love and kindness.

Forever Changed

Being the personal servant to the High Priest was a very important and privileged position, one that Malchus was exceedingly proud to have. He was very good at dealing with those delicate bits of business that his master could not directly attend to, but required an "official" representative to ensure that things got dealt with appropriately.

Passover was always a busy time, so much to do and organise, but this year it was even more so. That troublesome itinerant rabbi, Jesus from Nazareth, was back in the city again and stirring everyone up. Malchus had heard many things about this man. As the high priest servant he was also privy to many facts the uneducated crowds were not aware of. Although the Nazarene did all the miracles expected of the Messiah, he was not getting rid of the hated Romans. Instead he was denouncing the religious leaders and stirring up the people. This would not be tolerated and so the imposter would have to go.

So here, in the dead of night, he came to witness the arrest of this trouble-maker. He had often carried out these special errands for his master at night. But out here in the dark, outside the safety of the city walls, he was glad of the armed soldiers. They were following one of Jesus's own followers called Judas. Malchus didn't trust the man. How could you trust a man who was willing to betray his own master?

ENCOUNTERS

They were led amongst a grove of olive trees. In the dim light Malchus could see some shapes in the darkness behind the trees. They might be people hiding. For a fleeting moment he wondered if it was a trap, a double cross. But they had a large group of soldiers so that was unlikely. The commander had obviously thought of that possibility too, as he quickly sent some men out either side of them to flush out anybody hiding beyond the light of the torches.

Strangely though, one man was standing out in the open, just as if he was waiting for them. Judas hesitated, then went straight up to the man and greeted him with a kiss, the agreed sign. So this was the trouble-maker.

As they approached to arrest him, the man gently called out "Who is it you want?"

"Jesus of Nazareth."

"I AM he." Came the calm replied.

Immediately Malchus and all those around him staggered back, falling down to the ground in fear and shock. Though it was very unusual for a criminal to openly acknowledge who they were and wait to be arrested, it was the way the man said "I am" that made Malchus feel so uncomfortable, even terrified. The words were said normally but with such simple confidence and authority. For an instance it had felt as if God himself had just breathed out his own name as the Nazarene spoke. Probably the Nazarene was trying to work a spell on them. Whatever it was he did not like it and felt totally out of control. Like he was just a puppet in someone else's game. Most unnerving!

As they got up the man asked them a second time. "Who is it you want?"

"Jesus of Nazareth."

"I told you that I am he. If you are looking for me, then let these men go."

A glint of light flashing in the corner of his eye was the only warning Malchus had, as a sword swung towards his head. He flinched to the side and felt as if fire was burning the side of his head. Which was quickly followed by a warm flow down his neck, as he saw something tumble to the ground. It was an ear. He was cut! His ear was cut off!

He could not move. The shock of it stunned him. The world sounded muffled and distant, all lop-sided. The pain was intense but he felt numb inside and just stood there, shaking. Watching as the man they had come to arrest, bent down and picked up the ear, then touch it to the side of his head. Immediately all the pain went and sound returned.

"Put your sword away! Shall I not drink the cup the Father has given me?"

It was like a spell had been lifted and they could move again. Now they were back in control. The commander arrested the Nazarene and they headed back to the city.

But Malchus followed slowly behind them. No longer thinking about the importance of his role or his responsibilities. What was he to do? The Nazarene clearly was expecting them and yet he still chose to be arrested. Knowing for certain that he would now be condemned and killed. Not only that, the Nazarene had intervened when he was attacked and then healed him!

Without the ear he would have been maimed and therefore would never have been allowed to enter the temple again. He would have lost his job, his position, his status. But he had just been miraculously healed and so was free to continue to go into the temple and carry on with his job as the high priest's servant. Yet how could he after this experience?

It had all sounded so simple and right; what they had come to do. Get rid of this imposter from Nazareth before the Romans made an issue of it and started making examples out of everyone, especially the religious leaders. But now he was not so sure. He had experienced something when Jesus had healed him.

The power and authority that Jesus exercised was really real, unlike anything he had ever seen. The manipulative schemes and power games of the Sanhedrin and the Roman Governors were like a shadow compared with this. And for a moment while he was being healed he had also felt so loved and accepted by Jesus. Despite all they had come to do, there was no condemnation or animosity. Of all the things that had happened, experiencing this love was the thing that was most unsettling and profound.

The one he had come to arrest, had arrested him! It changed everything! Everything he had believed would have to be re-evaluated in the light of this one experience. He did not know what the outcome would be or where that would lead him, but only one thing he was sure of. He had just encountered a reality of love and an authority he had never known before and nothing could be the same again.

Based on Mt 26, Mk 14, Lk 22, and Jn18

ENCOUNTERS

There is a saying that 'ignorance is bliss', but then there comes the moment when we suddenly realise that we are ignorant, that we know there's something we don't know. And in that moment there is an opportunity of a choice: to choose denial, pretend ignorance and stick our heads in the sand – or to take courage and seek out understanding.

Have you been confident in your understanding about God but then suddenly discovered that the foundation of your understanding has changed and there is something you don't know?

Or something you felt you understood but then the truth you've heard makes you realise that you really don't?

What choice do you want to make?

Have you got questions inside you? Questions about what you believe about something, yet you feel unsure how to explore them? Perhaps, ask God where or with who you could really explore your beliefs and ask questions.

A Prayer of Blessing...

In the name of Jesus, I bless you to continually encounter and embrace Love, and so to be forever changed. I declare that you are free to make your own choice before God, for Love never forces but rather invites. I bless you with responsiveness to his Love.

I bless you with humility to honestly consider and challenge your beliefs, and the things you have understood to be true, in the light of

Truth. I bless you to know the One who is The Way, the Truth and the Life. I bless you with wisdom and safe relationships where you can explore the beliefs you have formed.

I bless you with courage to embrace the consequences of each Love encounter. That as Truth is revealed and lies are exposed, you will be able to step into the freedom that the Truth brings.

Epilogue

And so my friend we come to the crossroads, the final page where I must part while you journey on, but never alone. For I hope that during this time together you have heard anew for yourself the whispers of Papa's love, felt the warmth of His breath and the embrace of His arms holding you, and so have come into a new intimacy with Him.

Father, I thank you that you deliberately and continually pour yourself out, releasing love to all your precious children. I pray that they may know you better each day. May the eyes of their hearts be so filled with light, wisdom and understanding that they will be overflowing with an outrageous, joyful expectation in your wonderful goodness and everlasting faithfulness. May your mighty power flow gently yet powerfully in, through and around them, so that they become totally transformed into all you purposed for them before the creation of the world, as they partner with you.

Every blessing in Christ,

Peter

ENCOUNTERS

About the Author

Peter Waller was born one of four children to David and Margaret Waller in the mission fields of The Democratic Republic of Congo. His early life was lived simply and he would describe himself as "always knowing Jesus" since he was six years old.

To many Peter is known as a quiet and humble man, a faithful friend, a loving and trustworthy husband, a wonderful and fun father and a wise teacher and compassionate minister.

To those closest he would also be described as a man of immense passion… for God's presence, for God's Word, for prayer and, alongside his wife Karen and son Stanton, to see many come into the wholeness and fullness of life that they were created to live.

Married in 2011, Peter became a dad in 2013 and treasures the family God has given to him, seeing many reflections of the father heart of God through his own life experiences as a father. Yet, he also carries a deep desire to embrace, empower and father many spiritual children too. Alongside Karen, his ministry of wholeness includes; preaching, teaching, writing, mentoring and one-to-one coaching.